THE BEST
NAPKIN FOLDING
BOOK

EVER!

ADD EASY STYLE TO ANY MEAL

John + Stephanie Stislow

METRO BOOKS
NEW YORK

THANKS!

This book was a collaboration among many like-minded people. We thank them all for giving us the opportunity to create this book and for their experience, support, and guidance in producing it. (And for letting us sprinkle our personalities throughout.) Sharyn, Sarah, and Lynne at Quirk Packaging inspired us to bring out the inner quirk and add humor to all of our work. Nathaniel and Jen at Barnes & Noble brought this project under their wings and made it happen. Signe took the words out of our mouths and made them sound better. Christy and her creations were spotted at the right place and time, and the end result is a collection of beautifully crafted napkins that we can't wait to use at our next pig roast. And Eric, who we'd love to ZING here, but instead we'll thank for his camera and for being a constant source of inspiration in our lives.

This 2008 edition published by Metro Books
by arrangement with Quirk Packaging, Inc.

Folded, photographed, and illustrated by Stislow Design + Illustration
Text by Signe Bergstrom
Napkins sewn by Christy Taray
Fabrics for all napkins except those listed below are from Purl, www.purlsoho.com;
napkins used to fold Country Club and Your Highness are from Sweet Charity, www.sweetcharity.com;
fabric used to fold Tropical Butterfly courtesy of Christy Taray

Metro Books
122 Fifth Avenue
New York, NY 10011

ISBN-13: 978-1-4351-0414-3
ISBN-10: 1-4351-0414-5

Printed and bound in China

10 9 8 7 6 5 4 3 2 1

FOR THOSE WHOSE
LIVES ARE A WORK
IN PROGRESS.

TABLE OF CONTENTS

CHAPTER TWO
IN THE CUP..**48**

CHAPTER THREE
TO THE SIDE..**72**

INTRODUCTION

IT'S HIP TO BE SQUARE

Napkin folding is not just for geeks and grandmas—these days, it's hip to be square, particularly when you're throwing a party. Just watch any foodie television show and you'll see: a stylish presentation takes any meal, especially a festive one, to a whole new level. How can you get your guests to go gaga over your table setting efforts? Dig those crumpled cloth napkins out of your sideboard or linen closet, run an iron over them, and follow the directions in this book to fold up the coolest napkins ever.

Sure, it takes a little effort, but when your guests sit down to a table decorated with fancy napkins, they know they are in for a treat. A run-of-the-mill party is instantly elevated to a chic soiree, festive fiesta, or truly smashing bash with the simple addition of one-of-a-kind folded napkins. Well, it also helps to add some music, punch, and an assortment of your finest friends and family, but you don't need our help with that.

Whether you're hosting an annual holiday meal or simply throwing an impromptu get-together, *The Best Napkin Folding Book Ever!* is your go-to guide to folding creative, whimsical, absolutely fabulous napkin designs. Each napkin fold includes step-by-step directions paired with easy-to-follow illustrations and a fun photo of the finished napkin fold in situ. This book organizes the different types of folds by their ideal table placement—on the plate, in the cup, or to the side—to help you achieve a variety of stylish tabletop designs.

Featuring 20 versatile designs in all—from the Swanky Swan to the playful Tropical Butterfly and the utilitarian Cup Cozy, there's a fold perfectly suited to every taste and occasion. Each design is paired with a suggested party theme: the laid-back Cabana Boy would be just right for a fun summer shindig, for example, and the elegant Lady's Slipper would be perfect for a wedding reception or another fancy affair. Folding tricks, table setting lessons, and even directions on stitching up your own napkins from scratch are included in the Napkin Know-How and Expanding Your Repertoire sections. Throughout the book are helpful hints on everything from dining etiquette (page 17) to how to launder, iron, and care for your napkins (pages 39, 85, and 97).

Whether you make your own napkins or buy them, napkin folding is the perfect way to show off your creativity (even if you're not crafty). Not to mention, your table will be environmentally sound, while making your friends coo, your date stammer, and your in-laws love you. The centerpiece-worthy napkin designs collected here are sure to wow your most finicky guest, and transform the most mundane meal into the best party ever!

TRICKS TO FOLD BY

Keep these handy tricks of the trade up your sleeve to ensure a perfect napkin design every time. First decide whether you want to work with cloth or paper napkins.

CLOTH OR PAPER?

We dig cloth napkins (they're swanky and eco-conscious, too), but paper napkins have their merits.

- Paper holds creases better than cloth.
- Cloth napkins are better for flowing designs.
- A table set with cloth napkins is more elegant.
- Paper napkins are readily available in fun prints and wild colors.
- If you wanna go green, choose cloth; if you wanna take it easy, use paper.

WHEN FOLDING CLOTH NAPKINS

- Know your fabric. Linen folds differently than cotton blends, and silk is another beast entirely. By and large, silk is poor material to work with, while linen and cotton are both good for holding folds.
- Use crisp, freshly laundered fabric.

• Never underestimate the benefits of starch. Prior to beginning a design, iron out all the fabric's creases. If you haven't laundered the napkins with starch, use a light application of spray starch. When an intricate design is finished, a light coating of spray starch helps the folds stay in place. (Just be sure to double check the manufacturer's label on the napkins to ensure that they are starch friendly, then see page 85 for more tips.)

WHEN FOLDING PAPER NAPKINS
• Know your paper. When throwing a festive patio party, use paper with a fun, colorful print. A fancy but impromptu dinner party is better served by simple monochromatic napkins or a subtle print.
• Three-ply paper works best. Remember: The smaller and thicker the napkin is, the harder it will be to use for more complicated folds or multiple steps.

ALWAYS
• Work on a clean, flat surface and wash your hands before you begin.
• Work with napkins that are true squares, regardless of their size. Twenty-inch (50 cm) dinner napkins work best with these designs. Sixteen-inch (40 cm) lunch napkins will do the job, too.
• Press down firmly on each fold, unless instructed otherwise.

REMEMBER
• Practice makes perfect. Before debuting any of these designs, it's best to try the folds a few times.

TABLE SETTING 101

A casual, no-frills table setting may be your fallback position, but it's good to know the proper positions for silverware, place settings, and napkins. After all, you can't mess with tradition if you aren't familiar with it. Besides, you never know when you may have the opportunity to dine with the queen. Here's a table setting that'll keep you in her good favor. Tell her we say hi.

1	Dinner plate	6	Butter knife	11	Dinner knife
2	Soup bowl	7	Dessert spoon	12	Water glass
3	Bread plate	8	Cake fork	13	Red wine glass
4	Salad fork	9	Soup spoon	14	White wine glass
5	Dinner fork	10	Tea spoon	*	Napkin

UNCERTAIN WHICH SILVERWARE TO USE? BEGIN WITH THE SALAD FORK AND SOUP SPOON AND WORK YOUR WAY IN.

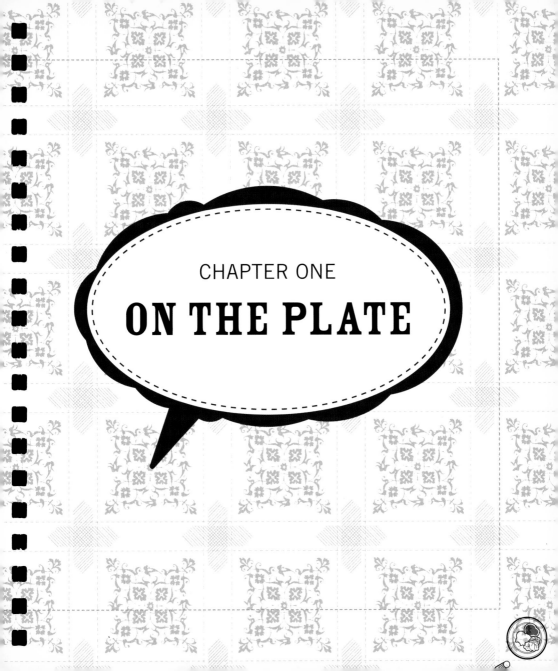

CHAPTER ONE

ON THE PLATE

COUNTRY CLUB

The Country Club dresses up dinnertime with effortless panache. Sleek and sophisticated yet decidedly cool, this classy triangle adds a sense of refinement to any evening meal. Just be sure to place the napkin so it points away from the diner. (You wouldn't want to put an unsuspecting guest on the spot, now, would you?)

1. Begin with the napkin laid out as a square with the pattern side down. Fold the bottom third up onto the middle third.

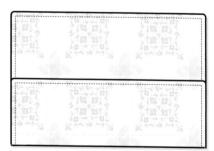

2. Fold the top edge down so that the top layer completely covers the bottom layer and the edges meet.

3. Fold the right side of the rectangle over to the left so that the bottom layer extends about 2 inches (5 cm) beyond the top layer.

4. Fold the corners of the top layer of the napkin under to make a point.

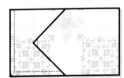

5. Repeat with the bottom layer so that you have two triangular points, the top one about 2 inches (5 cm) from the bottom one.

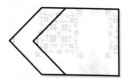

6. Fold the right side of the napkin under a few inches, but no farther than where the triangular points begin. Place on the plate with the point facing away from the guest.

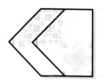

WHEN TO HOLD 'EM, WHEN TO FOLD 'EM

Napkin etiquette is so simple, you'll never have to gamble on a misstep.

- When seated, unfold your napkin and place it in your lap.
- After the meal, place your napkin to the right of your plate.
- Do not fold or twist the linen, as this is sure to annoy your companions.
- If you get up from the table mid-meal, place your napkin on your seat to indicate that you will return.

FANCY FISH

Thought to bring good fortune and ward off evil, fish are a frequent motif in Asian-themed décor. To create your own Shanghai soiree, pair this fish design with Asian-inspired treats, including nori-wrapped rice crackers, bite-sized dumplings, and fortune cookies. A whimsical addition to any table, this Fancy Fish will have everyone hooked.

1. Begin with the napkin laid out as a diamond with the pattern side down. Fold in half, bringing the bottom corner to the top corner to form a triangle.

2. Fold the bottom edge of the triangle up to form a strip 1¼ to 1½ inches (3 to 4 cm) wide.

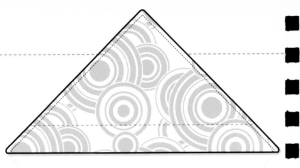

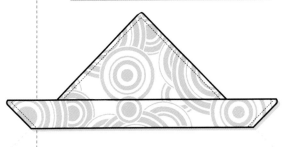

3. Flip the napkin over so that the top point is at the bottom.

4. Fold the the left and the right sides of the napkin from the center of the upper edge diagonally down to meet at an imaginary centerline.

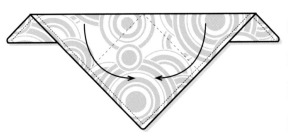

5. Fold the two pointed tips of these bands outward.

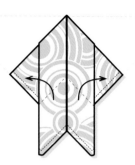

6. Flip the fish over.

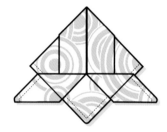

7. Arrange on the plate so that the face of the fish points to the right or left— your choice.

FISH, TO TASTE RIGHT, MUST SWIM THREE TIMES: IN WATER, IN BUTTER, AND IN WINE.
—POLISH PROVERB

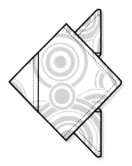

SQUARE KNOT

Like a good old-fashioned barbecue, the Square Knot provides no-fuss satisfaction every time. Because of its flat form, the Square Knot can double as a handy coaster for bottles or glasses. (It also makes an excellent Frisbee in a pinch.) Whether hosting an annual summertime grillfest or an intimate picnic for two, the Square Knot represents simplicity at its finest.

1. Begin with the napkin laid out as a square with the pattern side down. Fold the top edge down one-fifth and the bottom edge up one-fifth.

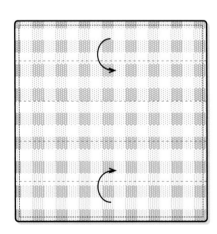

PRE-NAPKIN CULTURES, INCLUDING THE ANCIENT SPARTANS, USED HUNKS OF BREAD TO WIPE THEIR HANDS.

2. The widths of the top and bottom folded sections, as well as the middle section, will each make up one-third of the new height. Fold the lower third of the napkin up and then fold the upper third down on top of it.

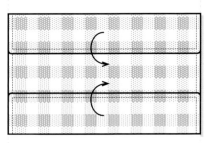

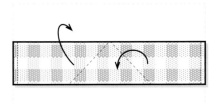

3. Find the center point of the top edge and fold the right side downward on a diagonal. Fold the left side diagonally back, so that it is underneath the central triangle.

4. Hold the left corner of the left band just below the central triangle. Fold the left band diagonally back, so that the excess rests on top of the right panel.

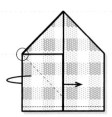

5. Fold the upper right corner of the excess length diagonally back. Fold the lower left corner of the right band diagonally up to align with the edge above it.

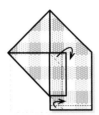

6. Fold the lower right corner of the right band diagonally up, and tuck it into the pocket made by the left band.

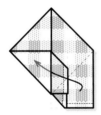

7. Place on the plate or use separately as a coaster. In a picnic basket, pack in between plates to protect them.

THIS IS YOUR LUCKY NIGHT

FORTUNE COOKIE

Every bit as clever as its namesake dessert, the Fortune Cookie makes a strong statement no matter the occasion. When setting the tone for a romantic evening, be sure to include a fortune or personalized message inside the folds of your guest's napkin. Unsure of what to write? "I love you" or "Will you marry me?" usually do the trick.

1. Begin with the napkin laid out as a square with the pattern side down. Fold the bottom edge up one-third and the top edge down one-third on top of it. The top layer should completely cover the bottom layer and the edges should meet, creating a rectangle.

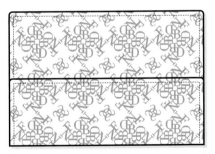

2. Holding the napkin at the center of the top edge, fold the right half back and pull down so that it extends about 3 inches (7½ cm) below the bottom of the rectangle. Repeat with the left half.

3. Fold up the two corners of the left tail so that they meet at the base of the triangle and form a new triangle with the point facing down. Repeat with the right tail.

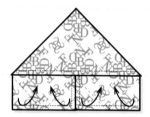

4. Holding the right tail in place, grasp the left tail and fold it over to the point of the triangle.

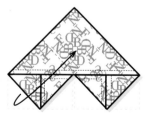

5. Grasp the right tail and fold it over to meet the top point, creating a diamond shape.

6. Fold the diamond in half by bringing the left corner to the right corner, making a triangle.

THE ANCIENT ROMANS USED A TYPE OF NAPKIN CALLED A MAPPA, WHICH WAS DRAPED OVER THE COUCH AND ALSO USED TO WRAP UP LEFTOVERS.

7. Place on the plate, propping up the napkin with the vertical slit facing you. For fun, insert a fortune into the slit.

JET SETTER

Evocative of a man's diagonal handkerchief fold, this design has "first class" written all over it. Its formal flair has the power to uplift even the most microwaved meal to a celebrated event. So, the next time you're sandwiched between two screaming tots in coach, fashion your airplane napkin into this lil' number. The steward may even reward your efforts with a martini or two.

1. Begin with the napkin laid out as a square with the pattern side down. Fold in half, bringing the bottom edge to the top.

2. To make a square, fold the napkin in half again, this time vertically, with the folds at the left and bottom.

AT MEDIEVAL BANQUETS, A SERVANT CARRIED A TOWEL FOR HONORED GUESTS TO WIPE THEIR HANDS UPON.

3. Beginning with the upper right corner of the top layer, roll the corner toward the center. Stop rolling halfway down, just before the roll extends outside the square.

4. Repeat step 3 with the second layer of the napkin, beginning at the upper right corner and rolling until you meet the first roll.

5. Repeat step 3 with the third layer of the napkin. You should now have three even diagonal rolls lying side by side.

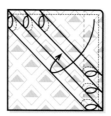

6. Beginning at the lower right corner (where the rolls end), vertically fold one-third back. This will hold the rolls in place.

7. Vertically fold half back, beginning at the upper left corner (where the rolls begin). Place on the plate.

TROPICAL BUTTERFLY

The Tropical Butterfly brings a touch of nature indoors and is a cheery accent for a springtime brunch replete with fresh fruit salad and vases of freshly cut flowers. Or, for a bit of fiesta-like flair, pair this design with colorful Mexican-themed décor and fare. The Butterfly may look like an origami masterpiece, but it's surprisingly easy to fold and sure to impress your guests—especially if there are kids at the table.

1. Begin with the napkin laid out as a square with the pattern side down. Fold the napkin in half, bringing the top edge down to the bottom edge.

2. Beginning at the bottom edge, accordion-pleat the top layer by folding the napkin back and forth at a width of about ½ to ¾ inch (1 to 2 cm) until you reach the top edge.

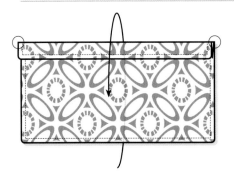

3. Grab the napkin at the pleated upper corners, hold them tightly closed, and then flip the napkin over so that the top edge becomes the bottom edge.

4. The narrow, folded portion should now lie below the lower edge of the napkin. While holding the center of the bottom edge, fold the lower left and right corners diagonally up to meet at the center of the top edge.

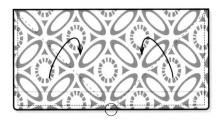

5. Grab the napkin at the middle of the top edge and hold the two pleated ends tightly closed. Flip the napkin over so that the top edge becomes the bottom edge.

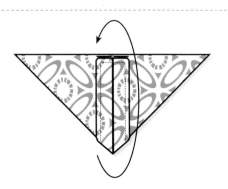

6. Fold the left and right corners diagonally up, starting from the center of the bottom edge, bringing them up to meet at the top. Slide the tips into the small pocket at the top.

THE KNIFE WAS THE FIRST PIECE OF CUTLERY; THE EARLIEST METAL KNIVES DATE BACK TO ABOUT 2000 B.C.

7. Fold the entire napkin down horizontally in half, bringing the top tip down to lie on the bottom tip.

8. Grab the tip that was just folded down and fold it up so that it reaches slightly beyond the top edge.

9. Fold the left and right tips of the napkin inward, overlapping one another.

10. Turn the napkin over. The wings will unfold.

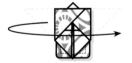

11. Make the body slightly rounder and narrower by squeezing it a bit. Place on the plate.

OUT, OUT, DAMN SPOT! COPING WITH STAINS

Although there are many ways to remove stains from washable napkins, it's most important to remember this golden rule: Act fast.

To treat a liquid stain, blot the excess with a clean white cloth, working from the outside in, before washing as usual. Do not press hard or rub or you may damage the fabric. For an oily stain, sprinkle with cornstarch and wash according to the manufacturer's directions. For dollops of food (like mustard), scoop off the excess and dab with cool water.

Keep an eyedropper filled with an all-purpose stain remover at the ready. Remember to test stain-removal techniques on a small area near the hem of a napkin before tackling stains in the middle of the napkin. For particularly vexing spots, there's no way to avoid it: You must take the napkin to a dry cleaner. Keep in mind that some stains won't come out. Permanent ink, after all, is exactly that: permanent. So, if you have ideas for a scintillating Hollywood treatment or bestselling novel, it's best to jot your notes on a paper napkin.

YOUR HIGHNESS

One of the most enduring folds, Your Highness has graced the tables of countless members of the privileged class. But why not turn tradition upside down and transform a casual night in front of the tube into an ironically formal affair? Your Highness will ensure that every guest—from the youngest court jester to the king of the castle—enjoys the royal treatment.

1. Begin with the napkin laid out as a diamond with the pattern side down. Fold the lower part of the napkin up horizontally just below the halfway point. The edges of the top layer should be 1 to 1¼ inches (2½ to 3 cm) in from the outer edges of the bottom layer.

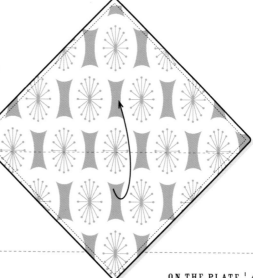

2. Fold the two sides diagonally up, beginning about ¼ inch (1 cm) from the center point of the bottom edge, so that the outside edges of the top layer align with the outside edges of the bottom layer.

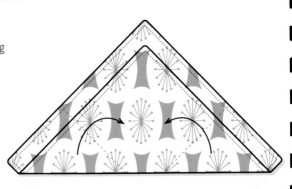

THE EARLIEST SPOON WAS MADE OF CLAY AND DATES BACK TO 5000 B.C. TWO-PRONGED FORKS MADE THEIR DEBUT IN THE 9TH CENTURY. THE MODERN FOUR-TINED VARIETY DID NOT COME INTO USE UNTIL THE 15TH CENTURY.

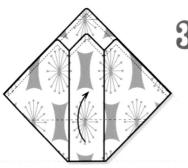

3. Fold up the lower part of the napkin up along a line slightly below the outside corners.

4. Fold the top layer down and in half.

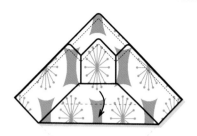

5. Fold the sides back and tuck one end into the other.

6. The napkin will now stand upright. Place the crown on the center of the plate.

CABANA BOY

More casual Friday than Buckingham Palace, the Cabana Boy is a staple for tiki parties and Hawaiian-themed pig roasts. Unconventional and whimsical, this design is a definite eye-catcher, especially when constructed with tropical-themed paper. Go wild and choose the most outlandish flamingo-and-pineapple motif you can find. Just be sure to keep your shirt on!

1. If you are using a large cloth napkin, reduce its size by folding each outside corner diagonally to meet at the center. Rotate the napkin so that it is laid out as a square. If you are using a 12-by-12-inch (30-by-30 cm) paper napkin, skip to step 2.

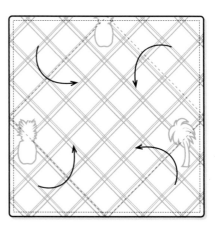

2. Fold the left and right edges in by one-fourth so that they meet in the center.

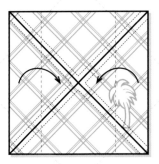

3. Fold the top edge back by approximately ¾ inch (2 cm).

4. To create the collar, fold the top edges forward on a narrow diagonal. Smooth down the edges of the fold well so that the collar stays in place.

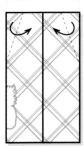

5. To create the sleeves, start at the center of the bottom edge and fold the corners of the top layer diagonally outward.

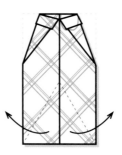

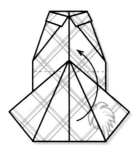

6. Fold the lower half up and slide the edge under the corners of the collar.

7. You can dress the shirt up with ribbons, buttons, or a lei depending on what the occasion calls for! Place on the plate.

"MAKE PLATE" OR "TAKE PLATE" ARE COMMON PIDGIN PHRASES FOR A TYPICAL HAWAIIAN-THEMED POT LUCK.

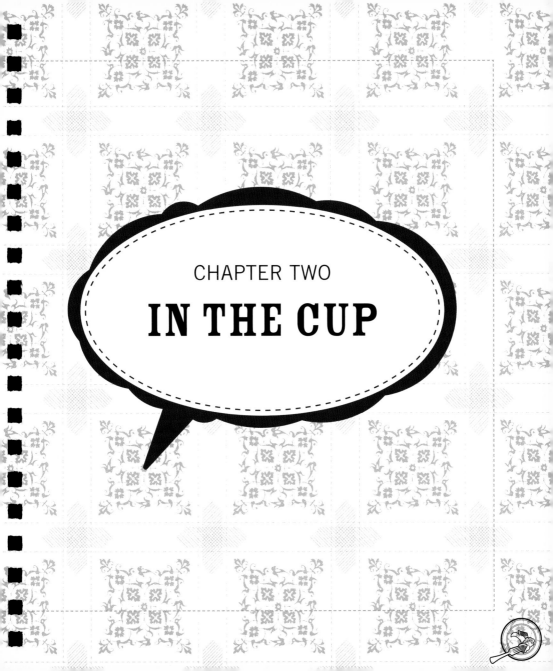

CHAPTER TWO

IN THE CUP

TULIP TIME

Adding a stylish touch to any afternoon cocktail party, this fresh design will have guests pining for their springtime favorites. Consider putting watercress sandwiches with bubbly bellinis or sugar cookies with lemon-mint mojitos on the menu. Perfect, too, as décor for an informal afternoon tea party, the Tulip Time would be sweet paired with an eclectic mix of vintage china.

1. Begin with the napkin laid out as a diamond with the pattern side down. Fold the lower point up about 3 inches (7½ cm) and crease along the bottom edge.

2. Fold the folded edge up about 3 inches (7½ cm) and crease along the bottom.

3. Continue folding up the folded edge in 3-inch (7½ cm) increments until you end up with a 3-inch-wide band with a point sticking up at the top.

4. Fold the final napkin point on top of the band.

THE FIRST PLACE SETTING, COMPRISING A MATCHING FORK, KNIFE, AND SPOON, IS BELIEVED TO HAVE ORIGINATED IN RENAISSANCE ITALY.

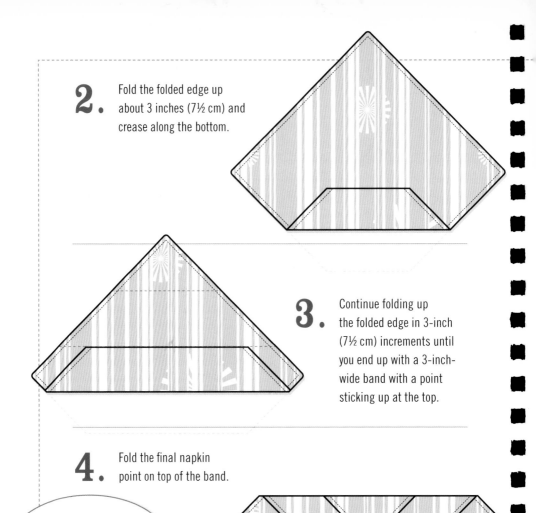

5. Beginning at one end, roll the band to create a roll about 1 inch (2½ cm) in diameter that is compact, but not too tight.

6. Leave 3 to 4 inches (7½ to 10 cm) of the band unrolled. Tuck the unrolled end into an open edge on the outside of the band.

7. From the top of the roll, working one layer at a time, gently pull up the inner layers of the band so that about ½ inch (1 cm) of each layer is visible. Place inside a glass.

HIGH-FLYING HUMMER

As fluttery as a hummingbird, this design replicates the appearance of its namesake in freeze-frame quality, allowing guests to get up close and personal with this otherwise flighty creature. To add a little whimsy to a ho-hum patio party, place High-Flying Hummers inside narrow glasses or vases. Who knows? Lucky guests might spot the real deal flitting around in your garden.

1. Begin with the napkin laid out as a diamond with the pattern side down. Fold the upper left and right edges of the napkin diagonally in to meet at an imaginary centerline.

2. Fold the lower tip up along the horizontal edges of the two flaps. The lower flap folds up neatly to form an isosceles triangle.

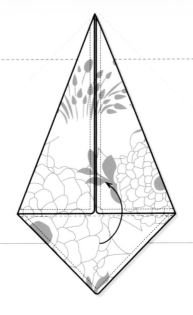

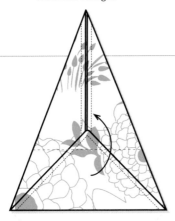

3. Fold the lower third of the napkin horizontally up, just below the tip of the isosceles triangle.

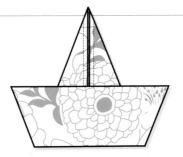

4. Flip the napkin over, keeping the upper point at the top.

5. Fold about 2 inches (5 cm) of the upper tip down, then fold about two-thirds of the folded tip back up.

6. Grab the two side edges just below the folded upper tip and carefully press them together (folding along the dashed lines as shown). The folded tip will begin to stand up from the table surface.

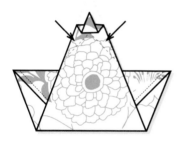

7. Fold the protruding tip over toward the left so that it lies flat.

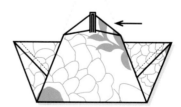

8. Fold the left half of the napkin behind the right half along an imaginary centerline, beginning at the bottom and stopping at the folded point at the top. The folded head should still be pointing to the left.

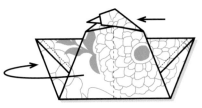

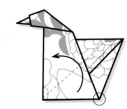

9. Grab the top layer at the lower right corner and fold it up diagonally so that its bottom edge aligns with the left folded edge.

10. Take the left edge of the flap you just folded and fold it diagonally so that it aligns with the right edge of the wing.

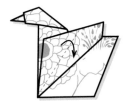

11.

Flip the napkin over.

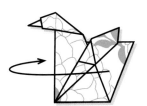

12.

Repeat steps 9 and 10 on this side, aligning the bottom edge of the top layer with the right folded edge, then folding the wing back down so that the newly folded right edge aligns with the left edge.

13.

Place the lower end of the finished High-Flying Hummer into a narrow glass, allowing it to open slightly.

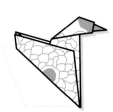

CUP COZY

The perfect nightcap for a cold winter evening, a Scottish hot toddy adds a festive feeling to any party. This Cup Cozy is a snuggly warmer for each mug that captures the Gaelic spirit of the isle. For guests who prefer a hint of the Highlands without all the malt, substitute cocoa, cider, or coffee for the toddy. For fellow countrymen, a dram of whiskey will probably do just fine.

1. Begin with the napkin laid out as a diamond with the pattern side down. Fold in half, bringing the top corner to the bottom corner to form a triangle with the tip pointing down.

2. Fold the folded edge down about 3 inches (7½ cm) and crease.

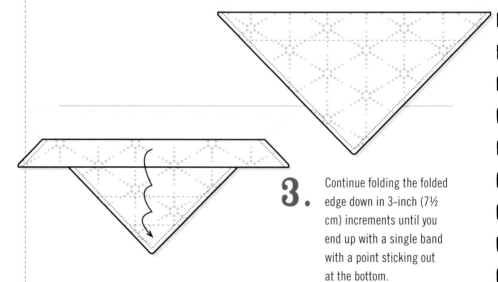

3. Continue folding the folded edge down in 3-inch (7½ cm) increments until you end up with a single band with a point sticking out at the bottom.

4. Fold the point up and tuck the tip of the napkin under the band.

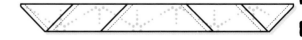

5.

Place the napkin around a mug, threading the left end of the band through the mug handle.

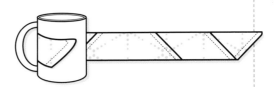

6.

Continue to wrap the napkin around the mug until only a 3- to 4-inch (7½ to 10 cm) tail remains.

7.

Tuck the tail into the layer closest to it to create a smooth fold.

"IF YOU CANNOT SWALLOW
A PIECE OF FOOD, TURN
AROUND DISCREETLY AND
THROW IT SOMEWHERE."
— ERASMUS

FOUR FEATHERS

Suggestive of a turkey's tail feathers, consider Four Feathers the official fold for a holiday dinner. Once you get the hang of the steps, you'll quickly fold up enough of these napkins to serve the entire extended family. Warning: An instant crowd-pleaser, it may prompt uncontrollable gobbling from Auntie Sue and Uncle Charlie, though they've been known to practice bird calls at every family function.

1. Begin with the napkin laid out as a diamond with the pattern side down. Fold in half, bringing the bottom corner to the top to form a triangle with the tip pointing up.

2. Fold the top layer along the dotted line shown, bringing the top corner down and across to just above the lower left corner.

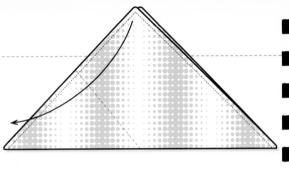

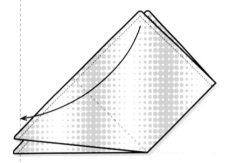

3. Still only working with the top layer, fold along the dotted line shown, again bringing the top corner down and across to just above the lower left corner.

4. Take both layers of the napkin and once again fold along the dotted line, bringing the center top corner down and across to just above the lower left corner.

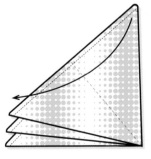

5. Holding all the layers together, turn the top right corner under along the dotted line shown.

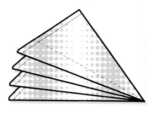

6. Fold the bottom point under.

7. Place upright inside a wineglass.

NEIL ARMSTRONG AND EDWIN "BUZZ" ALDRIN'S FIRST MEAL ON THE MOON CONSISTED OF ROASTED TURKEY AND ALL THE TRIMMINGS.

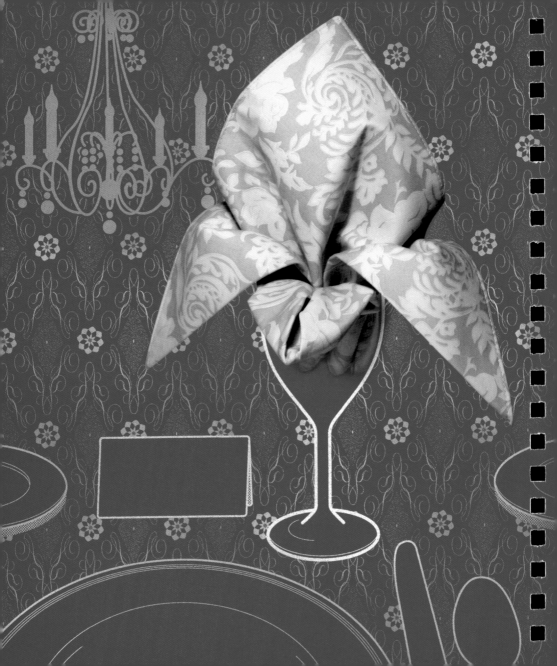

LADY'S SLIPPER

Exotic flowers, like the Lady's Slipper and other orchids, are ideal inspiration for napkin folders. Perfect for any wedding, this blossom is a natural showpiece, whether incorporated into the bride's bouquet or gracing the tables at the reception. A fluid interpretation of the live blossom, this Lady's Slipper design is sure to please even the most discerning of Cinderellas (or Bridezillas).

1. Begin with the napkin laid out as a diamond with the pattern side down. Fold to form a triangle with the tip pointing up.

2. Fold the left and right corners diagonally up so that they are the same height as, but slightly to the sides of, the top point. The left and right points should be about 2½ inches (6 cm) apart.

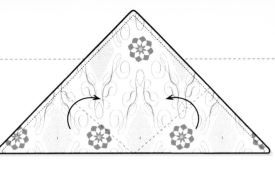

3. Fold the lower part of the napkin about one-third up.

4. Accordion-pleat the napkin into 6 wide sections of equal width. To make sure that the middle fold runs vertically through the center tip, first fold the napkin in the center, then fold the sides back and forth.

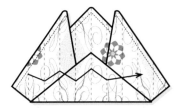

5. Hold the pleated napkin firmly at the lower edge. To unfold the Lady's Slipper, carefully pull the small tip in the front forward and down and then the two long side tips outward.

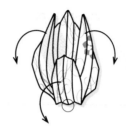

6. Tuck the bottom of the flower into a glass or napkin ring. Gently arrange the tips so they look like petals.

SPAIN AND ITALY WERE THE FIRST COUNTRIES TO ADOPT THE FORK AS A UTENSIL TO BE USED BY INDIVIDUALS AT THE TABLE RATHER THAN AS A SERVING UTENSIL.

IN THE NEW WORLD, FORKS DID NOT BECOME POPULAR UNTIL THE NINETEENTH CENTURY, WHEN THE ROCKEFELLERS, MORGANS, AND CARNEGIES ADOPTED THEM FOR EVERYDAY USE.

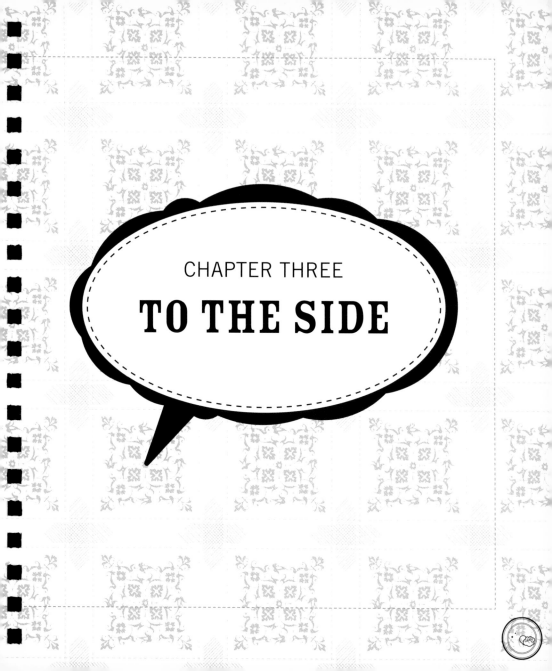

CHAPTER THREE

TO THE SIDE

SILVER POCKET

Hey diddle diddle . . . before the dish ran away with the spoon and before the cow jumped over the moon, the spoon, fork, and knife were a happy threesome. This simple yet dignified pocket reunites these essential utensils. A distinctive fold to use for special occasions, the Silver Pocket is also an instant upgrade from the kiddie table to adult company. This fold works best with a reversible napkin.

1. Begin with the napkin laid out as a square with the pattern side down. Fold in half, bringing the bottom edge to the top.

TRADITIONALLY, "CUTLERY" REFERRED TO KNIVES OR CARVING PIECES, WHILE "FLATWARE" WAS THE TERM FOR UTENSILS THAT WERE MADE FLAT AND THEN SHAPED, SUCH AS SPOONS AND FORKS.

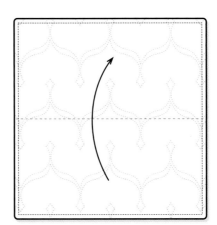

2. Horizontally fold the top layer down by about 1½ inches (4 cm).

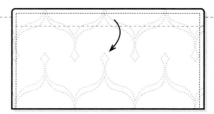

3. Horizontally fold the top layer down along the unfolded edge you've just created.

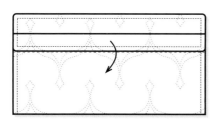

4. Flip the napkin over.

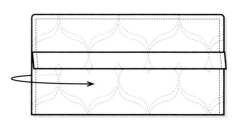

5. Fold the left and the right sides in so that they meet in the center.

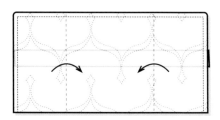

6. Fold the right half onto the left to complete the fold.

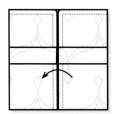

"IT IS ... UNMANNERLY TO SPRAWL OVER THE TABLE OR TO FILL BOTH SIDES OF YOUR MOUTH SO FULL WITH FOOD THAT YOUR CHEEKS ARE BLOATED."
—GIOVANNI DELLA CASA,
IL GALATEO, 1558

7. Tuck flatware, favors, or funny messages inside the pocket. Place to the side of the plate or in a basket for a picnic or buffet.

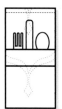

KEEP IT TOGETHER

Keep It Together is a common design for buffet settings. Its scroll-like simplicity is every bit as fun to unfurl as it is to roll up. Cleverly doubling as napkin and flatware holder, it's great for serving long lines of people with quick-and-easy style. Out of sight but never out of mind, guests' flatware won't shake or rattle but will definitely roll.

1. Begin with the napkin laid out as a square with the pattern side down. Vertically fold the right side in about 1½ inches (4 cm). Tuck flatware inside the folded edge on the bottom right.

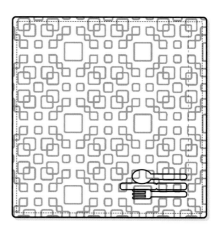

2. Vertically fold the left side of the napkin so that it meets the edge of the right side and completely covers the flatware.

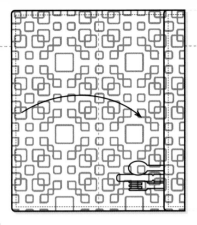

3. Carefully flip the napkin over.

4. Beginning at the bottom of the napkin, tightly roll the napkin toward the top, enclosing the flatware in the roll. Leave about 4 inches (10 cm) of the napkin unrolled.

5. Fold the top edge down halfway to the roll, about 2 inches (5 cm).

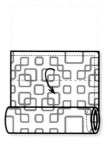

6. Complete the roll.

AT THE DINNER TABLE, IF YOU CAN'T THINK OF ANYTHING TO SAY, SIT QUIETLY. DON'T THROW ROLLS OR CHEW ON YOUR NAPKIN.
—*MASON COOLEY*

7. Hold everything in place with a napkin ring or tie. (Try making your own from ribbon or paper!) Place to the side of the plate or in a basket for a buffet.

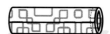

IT'S YOUR BIRTHDAY

Don't be mistaken—this ain't a dunce cap. It's got "party" written all over it. Remember the cone-shaped birthday hats from childhood? This grown-up napkin version is the next best thing to put a little mischief back in your merry-making. Play all the favorites: Twister, Pin the Tail on the Donkey, and, for the more adventurous, Spin the Bottle. Let the games begin!

1. Begin with the napkin laid out as a square with the pattern side down. Fold in half, bringing the top edge to the bottom.

2. With your right hand, hold the napkin at the center of the top edge. With your left hand, bring the top left corner down, toward the bottom edge, then turn it underneath the part you're folding to roll it into a cone shape.

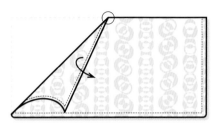

3. Continue rolling the cone toward the center, stopping the roll when the point (or tail) is centered at the back of the cone.

4. With your left hand holding down the cone, grasp the lower right corner with your right hand and fold up about 2 inches (5 cm) toward the top of the napkin. The fold should stop at the cone.

5. When you finish rolling, tuck the loose edge in between the layers of the cone. Fold up the loose bottom point, along with 1 inch (2½ cm) of the bottom rim. The cone should stand on its own.

6. Make a festive table by placing party hats around a cake, in the center or to the side of the plate.

WHAT YOU NEED TO KNOW ABOUT STARCH

Most effective on cotton or cotton-blend fabrics, starch adds stability to even the most elaborate napkin designs. Remember:

• Spray starch is the best quick-fix solution. If you're old-fashioned, laundry starch, in dry or liquid form, yields crisper results.
• After applying starch, iron immediately at medium heat. If the iron is too hot, the fabric will scorch.
• Spraying creases with starch will make them last longer.

SWANKY SWAN

Once the secret is out that you are a master napkin folder, guests will invariably ask, "Yes, but can you make a swan?" Wait for the perfect moment—during a casual brunch dock-side or while sipping cocktails aboard a yacht, for example—to debut this showstopper. Note: Choose a napkin made out of thin cloth for this design and use lots of starch to ensure that your folds will hold.

1. Begin with the napkin laid out as a diamond with the pattern side down. Fold in half twice, so that the folded edges are at the bottom.

2. Fold the side edges in diagonally so that they meet at the center.

3. Flip the napkin over, keeping the sharp point at the bottom.

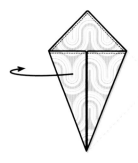

4. Again, fold the side edges in diagonally so that they meet at the center.

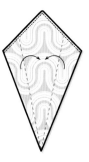

5. Fold the napkin horizontally in half, bringing the bottom tip up to the top tip.

6. Fold the narrow point of the top layer down about ¾ to 1 inch (2 to 2½ cm). This folded point will become the head of the swan.

7. Fold the napkin back vertically down the center, so that the right and left halves meet behind and the head remains on the outside. Smooth down the creases.

8. Firmly hold the napkin together at the bottom with your left hand, and turn the figure sideways. With your right hand, carefully pull the neck of the swan outward so that it forms a right angle to the body. Press laterally in the area between the head and neck to shape the head of the swan.

THE VICTORIAN ERA WAS KNOWN FOR ELABORATE TABLEWARE. ONE SET OF FLATWARE CONSISTED OF 57 PIECES RANGING FROM SPECIAL ASPARAGUS, BERRY, AND BACON FORKS TO BONBON SPOONS AND TONGS.

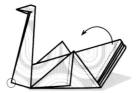

9. Continue to hold the swan at the base of the neck. With the other hand, pull apart the individual layers of the swan's tail so that they ruffle like plumage.

10.

Place to the side of the plate. Adjust the form of the swan.

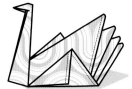

CHRISTOFLE MAKES THE MOST EXPENSIVE CONTEMPORARY FLAT-WARE. INLAID WITH DIAMONDS, A SINGLE PLACE SETTING WILL COST YOU AROUND $18,600.

TINFOIL SWAN

Want to really charm your guests? Send each of them home with a tinfoil swan containing their leftovers. Start with a napkin-sized piece of aluminum foil. Gently place the food in the pocket created in step 6, then proceed to step 7. Warning: Tinfoil swans are good for holding leftover turkey and stuffing, but are not ideal for soup.

GET LIT

From a cheerful twinkle to a somber glow or gentle flicker, candles provide the ultimate mood lighting. Used to signal a momentous occasion, holiday, or romantic engagement, this candle design is a perfect stand-in should the wicks on your real candles be too low to light. With its inextinguishable tip, this is one lit candle that burns the eternal flame.

1. Begin with the napkin laid out as a diamond with the pattern side down. Fold in half to form a triangle with the tip pointing down.

2. Fold up the bottom edge, forming a strip ½ to ¾ inch (1 cm) wide.

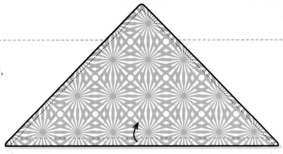

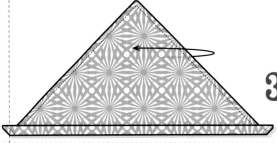

3. Flip the napkin over, keeping the tip at the top.

4. Fold the tip down so that it touches the bottom edge.

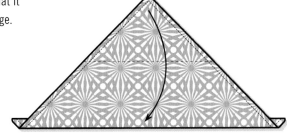

5. Fold the tip of the top layer back up, so that the point juts out ¾ to 1 inch (1½ cm) above the top edge of the napkin.

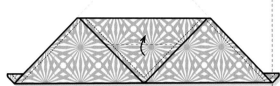

6. Fold the left side of the napkin toward the right. The crease should run vertically through the spot where the upper flap juts out over the top edge.

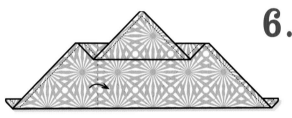

7. Tightly roll up the entire napkin from left to right, until there is only a tiny tip sticking out at the bottom right.

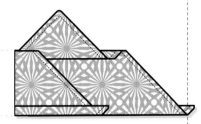

8. Fold this tip up diagonally and tuck it from above into the outermost layer of the napkin.

9. Gently shape the tip of the cloth to make it look like a flame. Place to the side of the plate or place all of the guests' candles in the middle of the table as a centerpiece.

THE EARLIEST KNOWN CANDLE-
STICKS WERE CAST SOLID IN TWO
PARTS, STEM AND BASE, AND
FASTENED WITH A SCREW.

DON'T GET FOILED BY THE FABRIC: NAPKIN CARE

With so many napkin fabric options, it's easy to get flummoxed by the various laundering instructions. The key to airing your dirty laundry is this simple:

NAPKIN TYPE	WASH TYPE	DRY TYPE	DRY CLEAN OKAY?
COTTON	Machine.	Machine or line.	Not necessary.
LINEN	Hand or machine, luke-warm water.	Line or lay flat. Avoid direct sunlight.	Yes.
SILK	Hand, warm water.	Line or lay flat. Avoid direct sunlight.	Yes, but not recommended.

Note: If possible, store napkins flat when not in use to avoid creases you can't shake. For tips on how to achieve crisp napkin folds, see What You Need to Know About Starch on page 85.

LITTLE SCHOONER

Whether planning an annual lobster bake or throwing a New Orleans–style crawfish boil, nothing wins over the crew faster than this Little Schooner design. To transform the maritime into party time, serve Dark and Stormy cocktails (2 ounces of rum to 1 bottle of ginger beer), sure to satisfy even the most dour landlubber. Irresistibly charming, the Little Schooner will get everyone on board. Anchor's aweigh!

1.

Begin with the napkin laid out as a diamond with the pattern side down. Fold it in half, bringing the bottom corner to the top to form a triangle.

2. Fold it in half again, right corner to left, to make a right triangle.

3. Rotate the napkin so that the long side of the triangle is at the bottom.

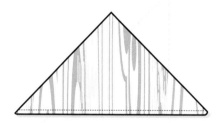

4. Fold in the corners so that the side edges align in the center.

5. Fold the right corner up so that it is flush with the bottom of the triangle, and tuck it behind the top layer of the triangle. Repeat with the left side to make a compact triangle.

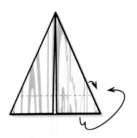

6. Carefully roll up the bottom edge to make a "hull" around the front and back of the triangle "sails."

"NOR IS IT SEEMLY...TO SPREAD OUT YOUR HANDKERCHIEF AND PEER INTO IT, AS IF RUBIES AND PEARLS MIGHT HAVE FALLEN OUT OF YOUR HEAD."
—GIOVANNI DELLA CASA,
IL GALATEO, 1558

7. Crease the bottom with your finger. Pass an iron over the boat to help it keep its shape; a bit of starch will allow you to stand the boat upright to the side of the plate.

FOUR-LEAF CLOVER

Four-leaf clovers have long been considered a source of luck, and for good reason—the odds of spotting one is approximately ten thousand to one. To improve your guests' chances of finding their own Celtic fortune, add these to your table setting. The quaint design is guaranteed to put smiles on your guests' faces—a lucky day for any host!

1. Begin with the napkin laid out as a square with the pattern side down. Fold the two upper corners in to meet in the middle.

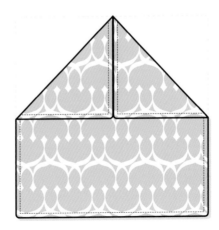

2. Repeat with the bottom two corners to make a diamond.

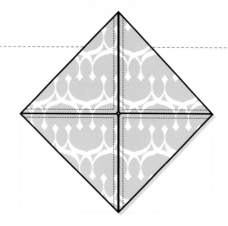

IN NORTH AMERICA, THE NAPKIN IS USUALLY PLACED TO THE LEFT OF THE PLATE; IN EUROPE, IT IS OFTEN FOUND TO THE RIGHT OF THE SPOON.

3. Fold each point of the diamond to the center so that they meet in the middle and make a square. Flip the napkin over, being careful to keep the shape.

4. Fold each corner of the napkin to the center again.

5. Holding down the center with one hand, reach underneath each corner with the other hand, and unfold the folds made in step 3. Gently pull the point of each corner's lower layer until the upper layer stands up a bit.

6. Fold the corners of the lower layer back under, about ½ inch (1 cm) toward the napkin's center.

7. Gently pull the upper layer's folds open, being sure to keep all the center points in place. Steam lightly and place to the side of the plate.

EXPANDING YOUR REPERTOIRE

SEW YOUR OWN NAPKINS

C an't find psychedelic print napkins for your swinging sixties reunion party? Searching for napkins in your family tartan? Buy some fabric and create your own. The results will be one-of-a-kind, and you'll save money that can be put toward other important party accessories, like booze. Here's everything you need to know.

SCORE VINTAGE FABRICS

- Finding vintage fabrics takes some time and patience, but the pay-off is well worth the effort. Search for inspiring fabrics at local thrift stores, vintage clothing shops, flea markets, and garage sales.
- Vintage curtains or tablecloths can be easily transformed into a set of napkins. The pieces of fabric are usually wider than bolts of cloth at a fabric store, so you can create lots of napkins from a single cloth. Just cut out any damaged areas and discard them, then follow the instructions in Stitch up Your Own Napkins on page 108.

HUNT FOR NEW FABRICS

- For a wide selection of fabrics, visit local fabric stores and quilting shops.

- Search online for unique fabrics at places such as purlsoho.com or reprodepot.com.
- If you come across crisp cotton or linen bed sheets or tablecloths you love, these can be easily turned into napkins. See Stitch up Your Own Napkins on page 108 for details.

MIX FABRICS
- For personality, mix old fabrics with new fabrics.
- Experiment with contrasting borders.
- Create reversible napkins; see the directions on page 109.

EMBELLISH WITH TRIM
- To dress up your napkins, trim them with ribbon or braid.
- Decorate them with new or vintage buttons.
- Bedeck them with beads.

ADD EMBROIDERY
- Buy an embroidery pattern from your local craft store or search online for a design you like. Most patterns are iron-on, which makes them easy to follow.
- If you like to draw, create your own design to embroider. Use a washable fabric marker.
- You can embroider a repeating pattern all around the edge of the napkin to create a border, or position a single design in the center of the napkin or in a corner.

STITCH UP YOUR OWN NAPKINS

What you'll need:

- 1½ yards (1.4 m) of 44-inch-wide (110 cm) cotton or linen fabric (medium weight is best, but lightweight cotton can be used, too)
- Ruler
- Chalk or washable fabric marker
- Scissors or rotary cutter
- Sewing machine or needle
- Matching or contrasting thread
- Straight pins

Note: Always preshrink your fabric by washing, drying, and pressing it.

NORMAL NAPKINS

Here's how to make a set of four standard napkins. Finished napkins measure 20 by 20 inches (50 by 50 cm) with a ¾-inch (1½ cm) seam allowance.

1. Using a ruler and chalk or fabric marker, measure and mark the dimensions for four 21½-by-21½-inch (54-by-54 cm) panels on the back of your fabric.
2. Cut out the panels with scissors.
3. To finish the edges, fold each edge back ¼ inch (1 cm) and press.
4. Fold all edges under another ½ inch (1½ cm) and press for a nice, clean napkin with no raw edges.
5. Using coordinating or contrasting thread, edgestitch (sew close to the fold) around all four sides of each napkin.
6. Press your napkins, fold, and set the table!

REVERSIBLE NAPKINS

If you want to mix things up a bit, select two coordinating or contrasting fabrics and stitch up these reversible napkins. Finished napkins measure 20 by 20 inches (50 by 50 cm) with a ½-inch (1½ cm) seam allowance. A turning tool will come in handy in step 6, but you could improvise and use the handle of a spoon or the blunt end of a nail file.

1. With the first piece of fabric: Measure and mark the dimensions for four 21-by-21-inch (53-by-53 cm) panels on the back of the fabric. Cut out the panels with scissors.
2. With the second piece of fabric: Measure and mark the dimensions for four 21-by-21-inch (53-by-53 cm) panels on the back of the fabric. Cut out the panels with scissors.
3. Position the front panel and back panel with right sides together, matching up the raw edges, then pin them together.
4. Stitch a ½-inch (1½ cm) seam around the napkin, leaving a 4-inch (10 cm) opening on one side and backstitching at each end.
5. Trim all four corners in the seam allowance, but do not clip your stitching!
6. Turn your napkin right side out, using a turning tool to push out the corners.
7. Fold the raw edges under at the 4-inch (10 cm) opening and press.
8. Pin the opening closed and topstitch a ⅛-inch (½ cm) seam around all four edges of the napkin.
9. Press your napkin and feature one side at your next dinner, then present the other side at the breakfast table!

Menu

Hors D'Oeuvres
Spinach Pie

Soup
Pumpkin Bean

Entrée
Roasted Chicken
with Lemon, mashed
Potatoes, Veggies

Dessert
Homemade Boysenberry
Ice Cream

NAPKIN DOODLE

After constructing more lopsided Tropical Butterflies and beakless Swanky Swans than you can count, you may realize you're more graffiti artist than origami master. But do not fret: You can create cool personalized napkins without folding so much as a corner. Impress even your hippest friends with Napkin Doodle, a postmodern take on napkin folding that requires nothing more than a paper napkin, a pen, and a sense of irony.

1. Begin with commercially folded white paper dinner napkins. Using your writing implement of choice, decorate the napkins with one of the following: (a) caricatures of your guests; (b) tonight's menu; (c) stupid jokes; (d) even stupider haiku.

RESODRCES

All Modern
800-615-9703
www.allmodern.com
This online retailer sells cloth and paper
napkins in midcentury-inspired prints.

Crate & Barrel
800-967-6696
Visit www.crateandbarrel.com to shop online
or locate a retailer near you.
Smart cloth napkins with coordinating placemats.

Gracious Home
1220 Third Avenue
New York, NY 10021
800-338-7809
www.gracioushome.com
Offers an always-changing selection of stylish
table linens.

The Horchow Collection
877-944-9888
www.horchow.com
From paisley to organza to crochet-border
napkins, this luxury catalog has it all.

Laura Ashley
800-367-2000
Visit www.lauraashley-usa.com to locate
a retailer near you.
If you want that English garden party look,
here's where to shop for napkins: striped,
checked, and floral.

Pierre Deux
888-743-7732
Visit www.pierredeux.com to shop online or
locate a retailer near you.
For authentic French country table linens,
look no further.

Pottery Barn
800-922-5507
Visit www.potterybarn.com to shop online or
locate a retailer near you.
Contemporary napkins and lots of other
tableware with a world beat.

Target
800-591-3869
Visit www.target.com to shop online or locate
a retailer near you.
Never underestimate Target's ability to deliver
cool housewares, including a wide selecton of
hip napkins, at bargain prices.

Velocity Art and Design
251 Yale Avenue North
Seattle, WA 98109
866-781-9494
Visit www.velocityartanddesign.com to shop
online.
Understated modern napkins for chic but
understated entertainers.

Williams-Sonoma
877-812-6235
Visit www.williams-sonoma.com to shop online
or locate a retailer near you.
Solid, patterned, monogrammed napkins:
whatever the host or hostess requires.

Yves Delorme
800-322-3911
Visit www.yvesdelorme.com to shop online or
locate a retailer near you.
Sophisticated table linens from a Parisian
designer.